Murder Weekend

Denise Kirby

Illustrated by Elizabeth Botté

Richmond ROBIN READERS

Published and distributed by

 Richmond

Richmond
58 St Aldates
Oxford OX1 1ST
UK
info@richmondelt.com
www.richmondelt.com

Created and developed by

International Language Teaching Services Ltd
Business and Technology Centre
Shire Hill
Saffron Walden
Essex, CB11 3AQ
UK
help@ilts.info
www.ilts.info

Series editor: James Bean
Text design: ILTS Ltd

This edition © 2012 International Language Teaching Services Limited and
© Richmond / Santillana Educación S.L.

This edition is for sale in all countries except Austria, Bahrain, Bangladesh,
Bulgaria, Germany, India, Indian Schools of UAE, Kenya, Kuwait,
Liechtenstein, Luxembourg, Maldives, Nepal, Nigeria, Oman, Qatar, Saudi
Arabia, Sri Lanka, Switzerland, Tanzania, Turkey, Yemen and the countries
of Central and South America

Printed in Spain

ISBN: 978-84-668-1646-5

Contents

The characters in the story

Milly

Hannah, her mother

Ed and Lizzie Halford, of Caves House

THE GUESTS:

Adrian Bennett

Susan Bennett

Clive

Penny

Brett

Anne

Damian

Charles

Two other guests

THE ACTORS:

Caroline, who plays Lady Dunsany

Andy, who plays Lord Dunsany

Polly, who plays Miss O'Halloran

Bernie, who plays Mr Rochester

Michael, who plays the waiter

Rod, who plays Detective Blakey

Chapter 1

Caves House

The first drop of rain hit the car window. It ran down the glass and disappeared. Milly looked out at the black sky ahead.

'It doesn't look good, Mum,' she said.

'No.' Hannah took one hand off the wheel and pulled a map out of the pocket in the door beside her. She kept her eyes on the road and passed the map to Milly. 'See if there's a village soon. I'd better get some petrol before the storm hits.'

Milly opened the map.

'Wakefield should be about four or five miles away. Then it's seventeen miles to Romney.'

'Oh, good. We turn off at Romney.'

Big drops of rain were falling now and the sky was even darker.

Milly looked at the map again. 'When do you think we'll get to Caves House?'

'About four o'clock, I hope.' Hannah glanced up at the sky. 'That's unless the storm slows us down. I remember the house is in a valley at the bottom of some hills. The road going into the valley's very steep and narrow.'

Milly looked at her mother. 'How old were you when you came here?'

'About nine or ten, I think.'

'And the caves were open then?'

'Yes. A lot of people used to go there.'

'But now they're shut?'

'Mmm.'

'Why?'

'I don't know. Those other big caves at Farnley were discovered about thirty years ago. Maybe everyone goes there now. I didn't even know Caves House was still open.'

Lightning lit the sky in front of them.

'Ah! Here's Wakefield.'

Milly looked out of the window at the shops and houses along the side of the road. The village was empty in the rain. 'There,' she said suddenly and pointed at a sign. 'Petrol.' Then she noticed another sign outside a small café. 'Oh, they've got hot chocolate, Mum. Can I have one?'

Lightning lit the sky again. Hannah turned the car into the petrol station. 'Okay. I'll have one too,' she said. She stopped the car and gave Milly some money. 'I'll get the petrol. You get the drinks.'

Milly got out of the car, pulled her coat around her and ran through the rain to the café. She heard thunder in the distance.

'Two hot chocolates to take away, please,' she said to the woman behind the counter.

There was only one other person in the café – an old man sitting at a table by the window with a cup of tea. Milly smiled at him. He nodded back at her.

'Storm coming,' he said.

'Yes. It looks nasty.'

The man lifted the cup to his mouth. 'Going far?'

'Caves House.'

The man put the cup down. 'Caves House?'

'Yes.'

'Why?'

'There's a murder weekend –'

'A what?'

'You know – a murder weekend. A group of people stay somewhere for a few days, there's a murder and they have to try to find out –'

'A murder?'

Milly laughed at the look on the man's face. 'Oh, not a real one. It's a game.'

The man nodded. There was thunder again, closer now.

'So, you're going to Caves House to play this game?'

'Well, no, I have to work. I'm helping my mum. She's making all the food for the guests for the whole weekend. She's a caterer. She's just started her own catering business.'

'Two hot chocolates,' said the woman behind the counter, and Milly turned to pay.

'Thanks,' she said. She took the drinks and started to leave. The old man nodded at her. 'Be careful in the rain.'

Milly ran back to the car. Hannah was waiting for her, and they set off again.

Ten minutes later they were in the middle of the storm. The sky was black all around them and the distant hills were lost in the heavy rain.

'Well,' said Hannah, 'it's the right kind of weather for a murder weekend.'

'Mum, who gets murdered? Is it one of the guests?'

'No, I don't think so. I'm not sure. There's a group of actors coming too. There's something about it in the email they sent me with the catering details. Look in my bag.'

Hannah's open bag was on the floor at Milly's feet. Milly reached down and pulled out some pages.

'Look, here's Romney,' said Hannah. 'We have to turn off here. There should be a sign to Hill End on our left. Watch out for it. I don't want to miss it in the rain.'

Milly saw it first. 'There! *Hill End 14*,' she read. Under it was another smaller sign. The letters on it were almost completely faded but she could just read them through the rain. *Caves House 17*. They were nearly there.

Milly sat back and opened the pages of the email. At the top of the first page it said ADRIAN BENNETT'S 40th BIRTHDAY and then there were a lot of details about the food Hannah would serve and the meal times. There would be ten guests and six actors to feed.

The last page was about the murder weekend:

Are you in...
The Company of Murder?

You and your friends are enjoying a wonderful evening in a grand country house. Suddenly there's the sound of a gunshot, and then a scream. You go to see what has happened - and your blood runs cold. That charming person who sat next to you at dinner has been shot dead!

But the weekend has only just begun.
The police arrive to question everyone. Who has done this terrible thing? Can you discover the murderer? There are lots of clues to help you during this exciting weekend, as well as lots of fun and laughter.

Join us in...
The Company of Murder.

Milly looked at the picture of a woman lying across a big bed. Dark blood covered the top of the woman's dress.

Milly closed the pages and put them back in the bag. 'It looks like fun,' she said.

'Yes. Well, just remember that we're there to work. I'll need your help making the food and you'll serve the guests at every meal. And you mustn't get in their way. Don't speak to them unless they speak to you. This weekend is really important for me, Milly. These people have plenty of money. If all goes well, they may give me more work. So you need to be –'

'– a good little servant girl,' finished Milly with a cheeky smile.

'Hmm,' said Hannah and glanced at Milly out of the corner of her eye. 'You just need to be charming, not cheeky. And do the job well. Okay?'

'Okay.'

Milly looked out of the window.

There was no farmland here. Trees and bushes grew close to the road. They shone with wetness in the grey light.

'The storm's passing.'

Hill End appeared. It was a small village – a few houses, a small shop, an old post office. A moment later it was gone.

'Nearly there,' said Hannah.

They passed a sign saying *Road open*.

Then, among the wet grey shapes of the trees, craggy rocks began to appear. Soon the road narrowed and the land on one side dropped steeply away. They were going down the side of a hill and Milly could see the tops of trees below. On the other side of the road little rivers of rain ran down the craggy rocks. Hannah drove more slowly and they wound their way carefully down towards the valley floor.

Milly looked at the edge of the road where it dropped away. It would be easy to have an accident here – to go over the edge and roll down and down into the thick, wet forest below.

'I hope we don't meet someone coming the other way,' she said.

Hannah was sitting forward in her seat, her eyes on the road. 'I wish the light wasn't so bad.'

'At least the rain's stopped.'

Suddenly Milly saw part of a roof below.

'Is that Caves House?' She tried to see more through the trees. 'Oh, it's gone.'

But before long they reached the valley floor. The road became wider and they crossed an old stone bridge. They passed a small cottage and moments later there was Caves House in front of them.

Hannah parked the car and Milly jumped out.

'Oh, it's freezing cold!' she cried and jumped back in again.

Hannah laughed.

Milly grabbed her scarf and hat from the back seat and pulled gloves out of her pocket. She put them on and looked up at the big brick and stone house in front of her. It was like something from a children's book. It had a steep grey roof with windows in it. And it wasn't square. Rooms jutted out here and there, each with its own little roof. It was wonderful.

Suddenly the front door opened and a woman came out.

Hannah and Milly quickly jumped out of the car and walked towards her.

'Hello,' the woman called. 'Welcome to Caves House.'

A man joined her at the door. They were about the same age, Milly thought – both in their sixties – but he was very thin.

'Hello,' said Hannah. 'I'm Hannah Foster and this is my daughter, Milly. We're cooking for the guests this weekend.'

'Come in. Come in,' said the man. 'It's freezing out here. I'll take you to the kitchen and show you to your room. I'm Ed Halford and this is my wife, Lizzie.'

Milly thought his skin was an odd grey colour.

They all went inside and Ed shut the door.

Milly looked around her. They were in a large hall. From floor to ceiling the walls were covered with wood panelling and a grand curved staircase led up to the floor above. The dark wood was beautiful, but after a moment Milly could see that the carpet on the stairs and the floor was faded and worn. She could also smell the dust in the curtains at the window beside her.

Ed pointed at a door on the right. 'Now, that's the dining room.' He pointed at two large glass doors on the left. 'And through there is the sitting room.'

Then he led them past the glass doors and down a corridor towards the back of the house. They passed another door on their left.

'That's the games room and library,' said Ed.

Milly looked in through the open door. There were hundreds of old books along the walls and comfortable velvet chairs to sit in. She could see that it had been a grand room once, but now the colours were faded and the velvet was worn.

The Halfords led them down a few steps to a lower part of the house and stopped. The corridor continued.

'There are three bedrooms off this corridor and the bathroom's at the end,' explained Ed. 'And there are three bedrooms off the other side of the kitchen.'

'The actors aren't here yet,' added his wife, 'so you can choose any of the rooms in this part of the house. They each have two beds.' She pointed down the corridor. 'These three rooms are a bit nicer than the others because years ago they were used by guests. The ones on the other side of the kitchen were for the staff.'

'Of course,' said Ed, 'all the guests this weekend will sleep upstairs in the larger rooms.'

'Do many people come to stay here these days?' asked Hannah.

'Not many,' he replied. 'Lizzie usually cooks for the few who do come. There's no other staff here these days. Just us.'

'Anyway,' said Lizzie, 'this is the kitchen. It's old but everything works. You should find everything you need.'

They followed her through the kitchen door.

Milly glanced at Hannah. The kitchen wasn't just old. It was ancient! It was like something from the 1930s.

'Um...thank you,' said Hannah and smiled weakly.

'Okay. Well, um...' Ed started to move towards the back door. 'If there's anything you need, you can find us in the little caretaker's cottage up the road.'

'Well, I –' began Hannah.

But the Halfords were already outside. 'We'll be back to welcome the guests at six thirty,' Lizzie called. And they disappeared.

Hannah and Milly looked at each other.

Hannah began to undo the buttons on her coat. 'Well, there may be two murders this weekend.' She looked at the ancient kitchen around her. 'Because if that stove doesn't work, I may kill someone!' She threw the car keys to Milly. 'Unload the boxes of food – and hurry!'

Chapter 2

The Company of Murder

'Oh, you horrible stove!' said Hannah. 'Come on, get hot!'

Milly was cutting vegetables at the big table in the centre of the room. 'At least the refrigerator is a bit more modern.'

They both looked at it. 'Oh, yes, wonderful!' said Hannah angrily. 'It's from about 1960, I'd say. Very modern!'

Milly went back to her vegetables. The weekend was beginning to look like a very long one – stuck in this kitchen with her nervous and angry mother.

'Where do I put the vegetable scraps, Mum?'

Hannah searched in a box. 'Oh no! I've forgotten the rubbish bags.' She looked around her. 'Look. There are some old newspapers in the corner there. Use those.'

Suddenly Milly heard Ed's voice coming from the corridor. He led another man into the kitchen. The man, who was very well-dressed, stopped and looked around him.

'Oh dear, this is a bit ancient, isn't it? Hello, you must be Hannah Foster. I'm Adrian Bennett. I'm sorry about the kitchen. I didn't know that it would be as old as the house!'

Hannah smiled widely. 'It's not a problem, Mr Bennett –'

'Adrian, please.'

'Adrian. We'll have all your meals ready on time. We're used to these small difficulties.'

Milly looked at her in surprise.

'This is my daughter, Milly, who is helping me.'

'Um…happy birthday,' said Milly.

Adrian laughed. 'Oh, yes. Thank you.'

Lizzie came in. 'The actors have arrived, Mr Bennett, and some other guests.'

'Well, then, I'd better go and welcome them. Drinks at seven thirty and dinner at eight?'

Hannah smiled. 'We'll be ready, Adrian.'

As soon as he and the Halfords had left the room the smile dropped from Hannah's face and she added, '…I hope.'

She and Milly went back to their work. But a moment later they were interrupted again by the sound of loud laughter in the corridor. A woman in a long blood-red scarf swept into the kitchen. Then came a man in a long coat, with a shorter woman who carried several dresses over her arm.

'Come on, darlings,' said the first woman to the other two, 'we'll sleep in the "servants' rooms"!' She loudly threw the last two words back towards the corridor. Somebody out there laughed. 'Mmm. Something smells wonderful,' continued the woman, and she swept over towards Hannah. 'Is it dinner, darling? I hope so. I'm so hungry I could eat a horse!'

She lifted the cover from a pan on the stove. Hannah just stared at her.

The man in the long coat smiled charmingly at them. 'That's Caroline,' he said. 'You'll get used to her. I'm Andy. And this is Polly, and we're the actors from –'

'– The Company of Murder,' breathed Caroline and turned dramatically towards them. Then she picked up a piece of carrot from the table and put it in her mouth.

Suddenly a young man in a red coat, an orange scarf and a yellow hat came into the room. 'Hey, has anybody seen my –?' He saw Hannah and Milly and stopped. 'Oh, hello.'

'And this is Michael,' said Andy.

'Hello,' said Michael and he jumped up to sit on the kitchen bench near the door. He grabbed three apples from the bench and began to juggle them. 'What's for dinner?'

Milly smiled at his cheeky grin.

'Nothing,' said Hannah, 'if you don't get out of my kitchen!'

But then another man walked slowly in. He was short and fat and without much hair. 'I've forgotten my pyjamas,' he reported unhappily.

Michael stopped juggling and grinned at Milly. 'Oh, dear, Bernie,' he said. 'I hope you won't need to go to the bathroom in the middle of the night. If you do, someone could get a nasty surprise!'

All the actors laughed. Michael started juggling again.

'Are there any more of you?' asked Hannah.

'Only one, darling,' said Caroline. 'But he's not arriving until tomorrow morning. He plays the police detective.' She dropped her voice low. 'We don't need him until after the murder.' Then she swept dramatically towards the door to the old staff bedrooms. 'Come on, everybody out!' she ordered. 'We must let...' She turned, looked at Hannah and waited.

'Oh,' said Hannah. 'I'm Hannah and this is Milly.'

Caroline smiled grandly. 'We must let Hannah and Milly continue their work.' And then she swept out of the room.

Andy and Polly followed her and Bernie went out the other door.

'Hey, Milly. Catch!' said Michael and, one by one, he threw her the apples he'd been juggling.

She had to be quick to catch them.

'See you later,' he said and jumped off the bench and was gone.

Milly smiled. The actors were funny. Maybe the weekend wasn't going to be so bad after all.

'Oh, no,' said Hannah. She was looking at her watch. 'It's late. You need to set the table, Milly. The plates and glasses are in those cupboards and the tablecloths are over there. Do it the way I showed you, okay? I'll come and check it later.'

Milly took the tablecloths and found her way to the dining room. Quietly she went in. It was a large room with high ceilings. It had some comfortable chairs at one end but most of the room was filled with a very long table. A big painting of some craggy rocks hung over the fireplace and there were lots of other smaller paintings on the walls.

Like the rest of the house, the room had seen better days. The table had marks on it and the curtains and the dining chairs were faded and worn. But you could see how grand it once had been. You could almost hear the ghosts.

Milly looked at a painting near a window along the wall from the fireplace. It was beautiful. She went to look at it more closely. A woman in a long white flowing dress lay on the wet ground. Her head rested on her hand. She looked asleep. In the distance was the shape of a man in a dark coat and hat. Behind him the moon had risen over winter trees.

The painting was very clever. It was beautiful but it made Milly feel uncomfortable too. She looked at it more carefully.

The woman wasn't sleeping. She was dead.

There was a sudden noise behind Milly and she quickly turned.

A pretty blonde woman said, 'Hello, I'm Susan – Adrian's wife. You haven't seen my husband anywhere, have you? I can't find him.'

'No, sorry,' said Milly.

'He has to get dressed for dinner,' said Susan and disappeared back into the hall.

Milly laid the white tablecloths on the table and went back to the kitchen to get the plates. She had to make five trips between the kitchen and dining room before she had everything on the table.

'Why didn't they build the kitchen closer to the dining room?' she asked Hannah when she returned from her last trip. She sank down onto a chair. 'My feet are hurting already.'

'Don't sit down,' said Hannah. 'You have to go and put on your black dress.'

Caroline swept back into the room. She was now wearing a beautiful long red dress, a bright necklace and a long feather in her hair. She looked amazing. 'Yes, hurry, darling,' she breathed to Milly. 'We're "on" in ten minutes.'

'On?' repeated Milly.

'Yes, darling. "On". On stage,' explained Caroline. 'Hurry. You'll be late. And I won't get my dinner on time. And *that* would be terrible.'

She swept out into the corridor and up the steps towards the hall.

Milly ran to change her clothes.

During the next few hours Milly and Hannah worked hard. But Milly had fun too. All of the actors were at dinner. They mixed and chatted with the guests. Caroline and Andy pretended they were 'Lord and Lady Dunsany' and everyone pretended it was their house. Michael was playing a waiter and he helped Milly to serve the drinks and the food. But he pretended to drink the wine himself and to become more and more drunk. He dropped things, fell over, fell asleep and had a fight with the feather in Lady Dunsany's hair. He was very funny.

The guests looked wonderful. The women wore long evening dresses and the men were in elegant black suits. Milly listened to their conversations while she served the food around the table.

'I'm glad there's a big fireplace in here,' said Susan. 'It's freezing outside. I think it may snow.'

'This is a wonderful house for a party, Lady Dunsany,' said one of the guests, a woman in a green dress with a large necklace.

'Thank you, Anne,' said Caroline.

The guest, Anne, picked up her wine glass. 'It seems full of mystery and ghosts,' she said.

'And dust,' added the man to her right. Everyone laughed.

Caroline glared down the table at him. 'What was your name again, young man?'

The man gave her a cheeky look. 'Brett, Lady Dunsany.'

'Ye-es,' said Caroline slowly and continued to glare at him. 'I shall remember that.'

Everyone laughed again.

'How long have you lived here, Lady Dunsany?' asked the very good-looking man on her left.

'Well, Damian.' Caroline moved closer to him. 'I may call you Damian, mayn't I?' she breathed at him.

He laughed.

Caroline sat back in her chair and raised her wine glass.

'Well, Damian, Lord Dunsany and I bought this house almost twenty years ago.' She pointed down the table at Bernie. 'Mr Rochester wanted to buy it too, didn't you, Mr Rochester?'

Bernie nodded.

'Is that a clue?' Susan whispered across the table.

But Milly didn't hear any more. She had to go back to the kitchen. When she returned they'd finished their food. Some of the guests were standing and one of them was taking a photograph.

'Hurry up, Clive,' laughed Susan.

'Well, move away from the fireplace,' the man said. 'Stand in front of those curtains over there. That's better.' He took the photograph.

Milly took the empty dinner plates back to the kitchen.

When she came back with the cake plates, Clive was in the hall on his mobile phone and there was a lot of noise coming from the dining room. Milly looked in.

Bernie and Andy – Mr Rochester and Lord Dunsany – were shouting at each other while the guests happily watched.

Milly put the cake plates on the end of the table.

Caroline – Lady Dunsany – jumped out of her chair and tried to stop the men. Then suddenly Polly, who was playing Miss O'Halloran, began to cry loudly and ran from the room. Michael came out from under the table with a bottle in his hand and followed her out.

'Don't cry, Miss,' he said. 'There's more wine here!'

The guests all laughed.

Lord Dunsany began to shout again.

'You're full of lies, Rochester. Get out of here!'

'Gladly,' cried Bernie and went to the door. He turned back. 'But remember this, Dunsany. I know your dirty secret!' And then he walked straight into Clive who was coming back into the room.

Everyone laughed.

Milly began to make space on the table for the birthday cake.

'I'm really sorry, Adrian,' she heard Clive say sadly, 'but I'm afraid I have to leave.'

'Oh no, Clive,' said a few of the guests.

'Now?' said a thin woman in a white dress.

'I'm sorry, Penny,' said Clive. 'I told you yesterday it may happen.' He went and put his arm around her.

'What is it, Clive?' asked Susan.

'There's trouble with this job I'm working on. The company's full of fools.'

'And they called you at ten o'clock on a Friday night?'

'No. That's my fault. I turned my phone off for a meeting this afternoon and I forgot to turn it back on. I just remembered, and there was a message.'

'But why do you have to go now?' said Penny unhappily. 'Can't you go in the morning?'

'Sorry, Pen. They want me there at six thirty in the morning and it's a two-and-a-half-hour drive. I'd rather go tonight.'

He gave her a kiss then said to Adrian and Susan, 'I'm so sorry, you two. I hope you have a great weekend.' He turned to go. 'Have a piece of cake for me.'

Milly followed him out of the room and he disappeared quickly up the stairs. She went to the kitchen to get the birthday cake.

Hannah was sitting at the table with a cup of tea in front of her. She looked tired.

'One of the guests is leaving,' said Milly.

Hannah looked uneasy. 'The food wasn't that bad, was it?'

Milly laughed. 'Mum, they loved the food.'

Suddenly Caroline swept into the room with Andy behind her.

'The food was wonderful, darling,' she said to Hannah. 'Well done.'

They all heard a car engine start outside.

'I'm glad it's not me driving up that hill in the dark,' said Caroline.

'Nor me,' added Andy. 'In fact, my work tonight is done, so I'm off to a nice warm bed. Good night, everyone.'

Milly picked up the birthday cake.

'Are you finished too, Caroline?'

'Nearly, darling. Nearly.'

Milly carried the cake down the corridor and into the hall. After a nod from Susan she lit the candles, turned off the dining room lights and brought in the cake.

Everyone began to sing *Happy Birthday*.

When they had finished, Susan said, 'Don't turn the lights back on. It's nice with just the light from the fire.'

Milly served the cake and waited in the corner to see if anyone wanted a second piece.

Penny finished her cake, took her glass of wine and went to one of the windows. She opened the curtains. Susan went and put an arm around her.

'Clive will be all right,' she said.

'But that road's so steep,' said Penny. 'It must be ten times more dangerous in the dark. He could easily go over the edge. And it's so cold tonight. There could be ice on the road.'

'He'll be all right,' repeated Susan. 'Come on.' She closed the curtain and they went back to the table.

And then suddenly someone was screaming in the hall. Everyone rushed in there. On the last few steps of the grand staircase lay the body of Miss O'Halloran, the top of her dress covered in blood. Lady Dunsany gave one more scream then fell to the floor.

The guests broke into nervous laughter.

'Oh, it's the murder,' cried Susan. 'I nearly jumped out of my skin!'

Milly, who was standing behind the others, silently agreed with her.

'Oh, look at you, Adrian,' laughed Susan. 'You're as white as a sheet.'

Everyone laughed. Then suddenly they all jumped again – an old black telephone on the small table next to Milly was ringing loudly.

Chapter 3

Road closed

Breakfast the next morning was at eight o'clock. At half past seven, Hannah sent Milly to the dining room to lay the table. Milly opened all the curtains and then stopped to look at the grey day outside. Light rain was falling and it looked very cold. Milly wondered if the road was still closed. She smiled. Last night had been exciting – the elegant guests, the dramatic murder and then the sudden phone call from Ed Halford to say that there was ice on the road and it was now closed. No one was allowed in or out.

Penny had immediately said, 'What about Clive?' and had taken the phone from Milly to speak to Ed herself. Ed had said he would call a friend in Hill End and ask him to look out for Clive's car. Penny had tried to call Clive on his mobile but there was no answer. And then, ten rather long minutes later, Ed had called to say that Clive had passed safely through Hill End, and the evening had ended happily.

Milly moved to warm herself for a moment in front of the fire. Then she laid the clean tablecloths and carefully placed all the dishes and plates.

When she had finished she stood and looked at the room to check that she hadn't forgotten anything. No, everything was there.

Wait a minute.

Milly looked around the room.

Something was different.

The painting that Milly liked, the painting of the woman on the wet ground, wasn't there. It was gone.

That was odd.

Milly went back to the kitchen then returned to the dining room with fresh coffee and pots of tea.

Adrian, Brett and Anne were the first to come down to breakfast.

'Good morning,' said Milly.

'Good morning,' said Adrian. 'I forgot to thank your mother for the wonderful meal last night. Will you tell her that we enjoyed it very much?'

'I will,' said Milly. 'Thank you.'

Susan came in. 'Good morning, everyone,' she called brightly. 'Have you solved the murder yet?'

'We haven't got any clues,' said Anne.

'Except that Lord Dunsany has a dirty secret,' said Susan and she poured herself a coffee. Then she whispered loudly, 'Milly, do you know anything? Have the actors told you their secret? Who's the murderer?'

'You can't find out that way, Susan,' said Brett. 'That's not fair.'

Milly laughed. 'No, they haven't told me anything.'

'Oh,' said Susan and reached for the milk. 'You haven't seen a clue or anything odd?'

'No,' smiled Milly. 'Except...'

Everyone looked at her.

'Well, yesterday,' she continued, 'there was a painting there.' She pointed at the wall between the fireplace and the window. 'And now it's gone.'

'Really? I don't remember it,' said Susan. She looked at the wall. 'Oh yes, you're right. Look, there's a square where the colour of the wall is a little bit darker. The painting must have hung there.' She turned around. 'It *must* be a clue. Oh, you clever thing,' she said to Milly. 'Well done.'

Milly smiled and started back to the kitchen. From the hall she could hear Susan saying, 'What was the picture *of*? I don't even remember it. Adrian, do you remember it...?'

Ahead of her in the corridor, Milly saw Michael coming out of his room. He was wearing his yellow hat.

'Hello,' he grinned and came towards her. He followed her into the kitchen.

Bernie and Polly were in there already and were helping themselves to breakfast at the table. Michael sat down with them and grabbed a piece of fruit.

'You were great last night,' Milly said to them. She turned to Polly. 'For a moment I thought you *really* were dead.'

'Yes,' laughed Polly. 'We like to give people a bit of a surprise.'

'They'll really get a surprise if Rod doesn't get here,' said Bernie unhappily.

'Rod plays the detective,' explained Michael to Milly. 'He's "on" at ten thirty but the road's still closed. He can't get through.'

'Milly, wrap these scraps for me, will you?' said Hannah.

Milly got a newspaper from the pile in the corner and put it on the end of the table. She went to get the scraps.

'Listen,' she said to the actors. 'I hope it's all right, but I told some of the guests about the painting.'

'What painting?' asked Michael.

Then his mobile phone rang and he pulled it out of his top pocket.

'Rod,' he said into it. 'What's happening?' He listened for a moment then said, 'Okay, see you soon.' He put the phone back in his pocket. 'The road's open again. Rod should be here in about fifteen minutes. So you can enjoy your breakfast now, Bernie.'

Bernie didn't seem to look much happier.

Michael grinned at Milly.

'What were you saying about a painting?'

Milly wrapped the scraps in a few sheets of newspaper.

'You know, the painting in the dining room. I told them it had gone.'

'What painting?' asked Michael again.

Milly looked carefully at him. Was he pretending that he didn't know?

'Isn't it a clue?'

'What clue?' laughed Michael. He turned to the others. 'Has someone changed the script?'

At that moment Caroline swept in and stood next to Milly. She was dressed all in green with a turban on her head.

'Who's changed the script?' she demanded.

Michael pretended to glare at Bernie. 'Bernie, have you changed the script?'

Bernie tried to speak through a mouth full of food. Everyone laughed.

'Milly says that a painting has disappeared from the dining room,' explained Michael. 'She thought it was a clue.'

'Oh well, we didn't move it,' said Caroline. 'Perhaps those two caretaker people took it down for some reason.' She suddenly looked more closely at the newspaper in front of Milly. 'That newspaper's five months old.' She smiled at Milly. 'The fifth of September,' she said grandly. 'That was the week I opened in *Romeo and Juliet* at the Cheapside Theatre.' She pointed at the newspaper. 'If you look carefully, you'll find a nice bit about me in there.'

'Really?' said Milly and began to search through the paper.

'Has anyone heard from Rod?' asked Caroline.

'He just called,' said Michael. 'He'll be here in ten minutes.'

'Oh, good. I thought Polly may have to play the detective and investigate her own murder!'

'Milly, this hot food's ready,' said Hannah. 'Can you take it to the dining room?'

Milly closed the newspaper and took the dishes from her mother.

After breakfast Milly stood alone in the dining room. She looked at the empty space on the wall. It *was* odd. If the actors didn't move the painting, then Ed or Lizzie Halford must have. But why? Perhaps it fell on the floor and broke.

She turned to go. Through the glass doors on the other side of the hall she could see the guests and the actors in the sitting room. The detective, Rod, was questioning them. He was tall and thin in a brown suit and hat. They all looked like they were having fun.

Milly heard someone coming down the corridor. It was Lizzie. She looked through the glass doors then turned and saw Milly. 'I'll make their beds while they're busy,' Lizzie said, and started to go up the staircase.

Milly suddenly ran to join her. 'Can I help you, Mrs Halford?'

'Lizzie, dear. Lizzie.'

'Lizzie. Mum's given me some free time.'

'Oh well, that would be very nice. Thank you, dear.'

They went upstairs and into the first bedroom. Like the rooms below it was grand but faded. Susan's evening dress lay over the back of a chair.

'Lizzie,' Milly said while they made the bed, 'there was a rather beautiful painting in the dining room last night.'

'Yes, dear?'

'But now it's gone. Did you or Ed have to take it away for some reason?'

'A painting?'

'Yes.'

'No, dear.'

'Oh.'

Milly pulled the bed sheet tight. 'So you didn't move the painting?'

'No, dear.'

'And you're sure that Ed didn't either?'

'Well, he didn't say anything to me about it.'

'Oh.'

They finished the bed and moved to the next room.

'Then where do you think it's gone?' asked Milly.

'What, dear?'

'The painting.'

'Oh.' Lizzie looked around the room. 'Maybe one of the guests likes it and they've hung it in their room.'

'You think that someone just took it off the wall and moved it?' asked Milly.

'Well, dear, I don't know. It can't have gone far. I wouldn't worry about it if I were you.'

Lizzie picked up a pair of pyjamas from the floor.

Milly looked around the room. 'The painting wouldn't be valuable or anything?'

Lizzie laughed. 'I don't think so, dear. Some of them aren't even very good. You'd only get a few pounds for them.' She laughed again. 'If you find a valuable painting, let me know. Ed and I could go on a nice long holiday!' She looked at her watch. 'Oh dear, it's nearly half past eleven. Won't your mother need you in the kitchen?'

'Oh...yes,' said Milly.

'Thanks for your help, dear,' said Lizzie and then she went to the next room.

Milly walked slowly back to the top of the stairs.

Suddenly, below her, the glass doors opened and everyone came out into the hall.

'Is it really necessary to search all the rooms, Detective?' Caroline was saying. 'My guests don't want everyone looking at their...things.'

The guests laughed. A few looked nervous.

'I'm sorry, Lady Dunsany,' said the detective, 'but we have to search the house from top to bottom. The knife that was used to kill Miss O'Halloran must be found!'

He started up the stairs and everyone followed.

Michael was at the back of the group. When he reached the top Milly grabbed his arm and whispered, 'Have a look for that painting.'

'What?' he asked, surprised.

'In the rooms. Have a look for that painting. It's a woman on the ground with a man in the distance.'

Suddenly Milly saw the detective looking at her. 'You're the cook's daughter, aren't you?' he demanded.

'Yes,' she grinned.

'Hmm...the kitchen – a very good place to hide a knife! I shall talk to you later.' And then he turned and disappeared into a bedroom.

The guests and the other actors followed him and Milly went down to the kitchen.

Chapter 4

The Halfords

'So you think someone's *stolen* the painting?' laughed Polly.

Hannah, Milly and the actors were having a late lunch at the kitchen table.

'Well…' said Milly.

'A*ha!*' Caroline said dramatically. 'You're beginning to see mysteries in every corner.'

'Come on, be fair to the girl,' said Michael. 'If we didn't take it and the caretakers didn't move it and I didn't see it in any of the guests' rooms –'

'Then where is it?' finished Milly.

'Oh dear,' said Bernie unhappily, and he took another sandwich. 'Who do they always blame when something disappears? The actors.'

Everyone was silent for a moment.

Then Rod jumped to his feet, put on his detective's hat and began to walk around the room.

'Uh-oh,' grinned Michael. 'It's Detective Blakey.'

'If you want to investigate this properly, Miss,' Rod said to Milly in his detective's voice, 'you're asking the wrong questions. The question you should ask is not "Where is the painting?" or indeed "Who took the painting?" The question you should ask is "Why?"'

'That's right,' interrupted Polly. 'My aunt has a second-hand shop and the paintings in this house are just the kind of things she sells. They're done by local artists or somebody's grandmother. They're not worth much. They're the kind of thing you could buy in any second-hand shop.'

Hannah stood and picked up her plate. 'Besides, even if it was the *Mona Lisa*,' she said to Milly, 'you are not to say a word about it to the guests. Do you understand me? Not a word. It's none of our business. I don't want any trouble. This job is too important to me. You know that.'

'But Mum —'

'Forget it!'

After Milly had washed the dishes, she went to her room and put on her coat, scarf, hat and gloves. Hannah came in.

'Is it okay if I go for a walk?' Milly asked.

'Good idea,' said Hannah and sank onto her bed.

'Do you want to come?'

'No thanks, love. I'm going to have a little rest. I'll need you back here at four o'clock, okay?'

'Okay.'

Milly went back through the kitchen and out the back door.

It was freezing outside. The wind was like ice. Milly pushed her hands into her pockets.

This was good. She needed some fresh air.

She walked around to the front of the house and looked up at it. It was a strange old place – out there in the middle of nowhere. It was no wonder that she thought something odd was happening there.

'Forget it,' she said to herself and began to walk quickly along the road.

The craggy hills rose up around her and the clouds hung low. She decided to walk to the old stone bridge on the other side of the caretaker's cottage. It wasn't far.

When she passed the cottage she could see Lizzie in the window.

It was odd. When Milly had told her about the painting this morning, Lizzie wasn't worried. She hadn't asked, 'Which painting?' She hadn't even stopped her work.

Milly reached the bridge and looked down at the water on the rocks below.

Maybe Lizzie didn't need to ask. Maybe she and Ed stole the painting.

Well, that was a silly idea. Why would they take the painting now, with a house full of people?

Milly looked up into the grey clouds.

And why was *she* still thinking about this?

The answer to that was silly too. It was because she liked the picture. Maybe it wasn't painted by a famous artist but there was something different about it. Something strange and beautiful. And now it was gone.

She looked across at the caretaker's cottage. Well...Mum had only said not to talk to the *guests* about it...

Moments later Milly knocked on the cottage door. Ed answered and led her into a small, warm sitting room.

'Everything all right up at the house?' he asked.

'Yes...Yes,' answered Milly. 'Except...I wondered...about the painting?'

At that moment Lizzie appeared. 'Oh, I completely forgot to tell you,' she said to Ed. 'A painting's disappeared from the dining room.'

'Has it?' asked Ed and looked at Milly. 'Where's it gone?'

'I...I don't know.'

'Well, I'll have to go and look for it,' said Ed.

'Later,' said his wife. 'After a nice cup of tea.' And she almost pushed him into a chair.

'Would you like a cup, dear?' she asked Milly.

'Um...yes, okay. Thanks.'

Lizzie disappeared into the kitchen.

Ed ran a thin hand through his grey hair.

Milly sat down.

'It's the painting of a woman in a white dress in the moonlight,' she said quietly. 'On the wet ground. Do you remember it?'

Ed thought for a moment. 'Yes, I think I do. Near the fireplace?' He smiled. 'You know, I don't think I've looked properly at any of those paintings for years.'

'Do you know anything about it? Who painted it? Or –'

But she didn't get a chance to finish. Lizzie interrupted with a plate of cake. 'Have a piece of cake, dear. The tea's nearly ready.'

Ed stood up. 'No, I don't know anything about the painting,' he said. 'But I do know that before he died, my father made a complete list of everything in that house. It's in a green book somewhere.'

'You're not going to look for it now, are you?' said Lizzie. She looked worried.

'Was your father the caretaker here too?' asked Milly.

Ed and Lizzie smiled at each other.

'We live in the caretaker's cottage because we only need a small place,' replied Ed, 'but we're not caretakers – we're the owners.'

Milly was surprised. 'You own Caves House?'

'Yes. And everything in it.'

Milly let out her breath. That meant the Halfords didn't take the painting. After all, you can't steal from yourself.

'Not that the house is worth much,' continued Ed. 'We've tried to sell it but nobody wants to buy it. Why would they? Hardly anyone comes here these days. They all go to see the caves at Farnley.'

'So you've lived here all your life?' asked Milly.

'No,' said Ed. 'No, my mother left my father when I was very young and she took me to live in Australia. I didn't come back here until about twenty-five years ago. And then my father died and I got the house. I still have a few of his things in the bedroom. The list should be there.'

'Oh, forget about it, Ed,' said Lizzie.

But he was gone.

Milly looked at her. Lizzie didn't seem to want to talk about the painting. Why?

Lizzie saw the question in her eyes.

'It's Ed, dear,' she said quietly. 'I don't want him to worry about anything. He's not well, you see.' A tear appeared at the corner of her eye. 'In fact, he's very ill.'

'Oh, Lizzie,' said Milly immediately. 'I'm sorry.'

'So I don't want him to worry about anything. Especially not about that house or anything in it. It's been enough trouble already. We can't sell it but it doesn't make much money for us. Ed should be living somewhere warmer. But we don't have the money to move. We're stuck here.' She stood up. 'I'd better get that tea.' And she went into the kitchen.

Milly waited.

Ed came back into the sitting room with an old book with a green cloth cover. 'I knew I'd find it,' he said. 'Here it is.'

He sat down next to Milly and began to turn the pages.

'Here we are.' He stopped at a page marked *Paintings*.

There was a list of about fifty paintings. Some had a name while others had only a description. Some of them had the artist's name as well.

Milly looked down the list. Would she recognise the painting by its name?

Ed pointed to one. '*Lady by the Lake*? Is that it?'

'No, I don't think so.'

Then suddenly Milly pointed at another name on the list.

'There! That's it! I'm sure that's the one. I'm sure that's the name.'

'*Murder in the Moonlight*,' read Ed, 'painted by Isadore Richmond.'

Milly suddenly stood up. 'But that's...' She turned to Ed. 'I have to check something.' She started to go. 'I have to check something!'

'What?' called Ed.

But Milly was already running up the road towards Caves House.

Isadore Richmond! She had seen that name before. And if she was right...

She ran around to the back of the house and threw open the back door. She was breathing hard.

Hannah, who was in the kitchen, stared at her in surprise. 'What's wrong? What's happened?'

Milly looked at the table. She tried to catch her breath. 'Where's the newspaper...that I was reading...this morning?'

'The old one?' asked Hannah. 'What –?'

'Yes,' interrupted Milly. 'Where is it?'

Hannah looked around her. 'Well, I...I think I wrapped the rubbish in it.'

Milly hurried back outside and over to a metal bin that stood not far away. She threw the cover of the bin onto the ground and started pulling out pieces of newspaper.

'What *are* you doing?' asked Hannah at the door.

Milly didn't answer. She took out each sheet of newspaper, searched both sides of it and then threw it away and grabbed another one.

Then suddenly she stopped. Excitedly she held up a wet, torn and dirty piece of paper. 'Here it is!' she said. 'Listen! *Local Artist Has Life After Death.*'

'What?' asked Hannah.

But Milly continued to read aloud. '*The artist, Isadore Richmond, who died three months ago at the age of eighty-seven, lived most of his life in Italy. But it may surprise many people to learn that he was born, and lived the first twenty-seven years of his life, here in Romney. The art world has certainly been surprised by the prices of Richmond's paintings since his death. A work he painted in 1987,* Careless, *sold yesterday in London for £198,000!*'

Chapter 5

Someone in the room

'I don't believe this!' cried Hannah. 'I don't believe it!' She looked down at Milly, who sat unhappily at the kitchen table. 'I told you to forget about it. And what do you do? You go digging around until you find this…this Isadore Richmond!' She threw the sheet of newspaper on the table. 'And what's going to happen now? Well, now you're going to ruin everybody's weekend, aren't you? And ruin any chance I had to get another job from these people. Well done!'

'Mum, the Halfords think the painting isn't worth anything. But it *is*. I'm not sorry I found out about it. It could change their lives. Besides we can't just let the thief escape. I'm sorry about the catering job but we have to tell the Halfords.'

'Tell the Halfords what?' Ed and Lizzie stood at the door.

Milly slowly stood up and showed them the story in the newspaper. 'I think someone's taken the painting because they know it could be worth a lot of money.'

Ed and Lizzie read the story and then Ed sat down, the newspaper still in his hand. 'A hundred and ninety-eight thousand pounds!' he said in wonder. 'I don't believe it!'

'Well, that is a surprise,' said Lizzie.

Ed turned to Milly. 'And you say the painting was there yesterday evening but it was gone this morning?'

'That's right.' Milly looked at Hannah then back at the Halfords. 'What are you going to do?'

'Oh dear,' said Lizzie. 'We can't ruin Mr Bennett's birthday party. They all seem to be very nice people. I'm sure none of them has taken the painting.'

'The actors seem really nice too,' said Milly gently.

'Yes,' said Ed and he put his head in his hands.

Lizzie put a hand on his back. 'Don't you worry about it,

Ed. We'll get the police to come and they can investigate it.'

Ed smiled up at her. 'Now that would really ruin the weekend. No.' He looked up at Hannah. 'What are the guests doing this afternoon?'

'The actors have brought them together in the sitting room. The detective is questioning them about the murder again. I have to serve tea at four o'clock.'

Ed looked at his watch. 'That gives us nearly an hour. Are you sure they're all in there?' he asked Hannah.

'Yes, I think so. Oh, except Polly, the actor who was murdered last night. I saw her earlier going for a walk.'

'Right,' said Ed. 'Hannah, you need to make the afternoon tea. But may we borrow Milly to help us search the rooms?'

'Search the rooms?' repeated Milly, her eyes wide.

Ed stood up. 'If we find the painting, we may find the thief. And, instead of accusing everyone, we can talk to that one person, quietly. If it turns out to be one of the actors, the guests need never know.'

Hannah smiled at that. 'Okay,' she said. 'But be careful.'

'We'll look in the actor's rooms first,' said Ed. 'And we'll stay near each other. If you have a problem, Milly, just call.'

Thirty minutes later, Milly was moving silently about one of the rooms. She looked under the bed, inside the cupboards and behind the curtains. Going from room to room like this felt strange. The old house seemed to be watching her. She jumped at every small sound it made. She was glad this was the last room she had to search.

There was a blue case against the wall. She looked at it uncomfortably. She didn't want to open it. Searching through other people's things wasn't nice. Most of the bags in the other rooms had been too small to hold the painting – the painting wasn't large but it wasn't small either – so she hadn't looked inside them. But it could just fit in that case.

Milly crept over and laid the case on the floor. There was a name on the top edge – *Penny Harrington*. Carefully Milly opened it.

Suddenly a sharp voice behind her cut through the silence. 'What *do* you think you're doing?'

'The girl had her hands in my case!' cried Penny. 'And now you tell us that you've been in *everybody's* room?'

The guests on one side of the sitting room stared at Ed, Lizzie and Milly on the other side. The actors stood together near the fireplace.

'Oh dear,' said Lizzie.

Ed sat down. 'We hoped we wouldn't have to tell you all.'

'Tell us what?' asked Adrian.

Ed didn't look well. Lizzie went to his side.

'About the painting that disappeared from the dining room,' answered Milly. 'It wasn't a clue in the murder weekend. But someone has taken it – for another reason. We found out that the artist who painted it is Isadore Richmond.'

'Who?' said Penny.

'He's an artist who died earlier this year. And since his death, his work has become rather valuable. One of his paintings sold a few months ago for one hundred and ninety-eight thousand pounds.'

There was complete silence for a moment.

Then Brett said, 'And I thought this place was full of dust and rubbish!'

The other guests laughed.

'Wait a minute,' said Adrian. 'Are you saying that you think one of *us* stole the painting?'

Everyone looked at Milly and the Halfords.

'Well...' began Milly, but then she couldn't find the words.

'Have you been searching for the painting in our rooms?' demanded Penny.

'Yes,' said Ed quietly.

'I don't believe it!' She pointed at the other guests. 'You think one of *us* took the painting? How ridiculous!' She laughed and turned toward the actors. 'Did you search their rooms too?'

'Careful, Pen,' said Adrian.

'Oh dear,' said Bernie.

'Look,' said Ed. 'We didn't want to cause any trouble. I know we shouldn't have been in the rooms. But we thought that if we could find the painting, we could keep the whole thing quiet and it wouldn't ruin the weekend for everyone.'

Penny glared. 'Well, that didn't happen, did it?'

'So you searched all the rooms?' asked Adrian quietly.

'Yes,' answered Ed.

'And did you find the painting?'

'No.'

'Hah!' said Penny. 'There you are! None of us took it. I told you this was ridiculous.'

'I don't think that's the point, Pen,' said Susan softly.

Ed moved uncomfortably in his chair. 'Did anyone see anybody else in or around the house yesterday evening or this morning?'

Everyone looked at one another.

'No.'

'No.'

'No one.'

'I see,' said Ed. And the room went quiet.

'What are you saying?' asked Penny.

Milly said, 'I saw the painting on the wall at about six o'clock yesterday evening and I noticed it had gone at about seven thirty this morning. Someone must have taken it between those hours.'

'But anyone could have come into the house after dark,' said Brett.

'No,' said Adrian. 'I'm afraid they couldn't. Unless they broke in. Ed gave me the keys yesterday and I locked the doors after dinner. Is there any sign of anyone trying to break in?'

'No,' said Ed.

'So...' said Penny and slowly sank down onto the chair behind her. 'So, it *must* have been taken by someone who's in this room.'

At that moment Hannah appeared at the glass doors. 'Are you ready for afternoon –?' she began, but stopped when she saw Milly and the Halfords there.

Rod dropped his detective's hat onto the back of a chair, sat down and crossed his legs. 'Well, it wasn't me,' he said happily. 'I didn't arrive here until nearly ten o'clock this morning.'

'Good for you,' said Brett rather nastily. 'But wait a minute. Someone's not here. Where's the girl who was murdered last night?'

'Her name's Polly,' said Caroline with a tight smile.

'She's in the kitchen,' said Hannah. 'I'll get her.'

Penny said, 'Well, it wasn't me. I've never heard of this... Isadore person. It wasn't any of us.' She looked at her friends.

'That's right,' added Damian. 'I mean, to be honest, none of us needs the money. I mean, I know one hundred and ninety-eight thousand pounds sounds like a lot of money but –'

Caroline finished his sentence. '...but if you're *wealthy*,' she said slowly and carefully, 'it's a very small amount. For the rest of us, it's a rather large mountain of money. Thank you for pointing that out.' The smile never left her face.

Hannah came back in with Polly.

'Hey, Polly,' said Rod brightly, 'come and sit over here with the rest of the thieves.'

'I didn't say –' started Damian.

But Rod stopped him. 'You know, someone else isn't here.' He turned to the other actors. 'Didn't you say one of the guests left last night?'

Penny was immediately angry. 'Are you accusing Clive? Clive doesn't need to steal a painting! Anyway, we were all in the dining room. We saw him drive away and the painting was still on the wall.' She looked up at her friends. 'Wasn't it?'

'I can't remember the painting at all,' said Adrian.

'Wait a minute,' said Susan and picked up a camera from the low table in front of her. She turned it on and pushed a button on the back of it a few times. 'Clive took some photographs of us near the fireplace last night. Remember? Yes, look.' She brought the camera over to Milly and showed her a photograph. 'Is that the painting?'

Behind the group of happy faces *Murder in the Moonlight* was hanging on the wall.

'Yes,' said Milly.

'There you are,' said Penny happily. 'The painting was still there when Clive left.' She looked at Rod.

'So,' said Rod with a cheeky grin, 'it wasn't me and it wasn't Clive.' He put his hands behind his head and rested back against the chair. 'Now what do we do?'

Ed slowly stood up. 'I'm afraid I'm going to have to call the police.'

'Oh dear,' said Bernie.

Ed and Lizzie went to the phone in the hall.

Everyone looked at each other in an uncomfortable silence.

'This is ridiculous!' said Penny. She stood up, and then sat down again.

Caroline sat down and said, 'Anyone else hungry?'

'Yes,' said Adrian to Hannah. 'Perhaps you'd better serve the afternoon tea.'

Hannah grabbed Milly's arm and was leading her out of the room when Ed and Lizzie returned.

'They've closed the road again,' Ed told everyone. 'The police can't come until it's open, in the morning. They've asked that no one leaves the house before then.'

Chapter 6

In the night

Michael caught up with Milly in the dark corridor.

'I'm so glad that's the end of dinner!' he said. 'I've never felt so uncomfortable in my life. Adrian thought that if we continued the murder weekend, it would give everyone a laugh. But it just made things worse. Every time someone said the word "investigate" or "discover" or "clues" the whole room went quiet.'

'I know,' said Milly. 'It was horrible.'

They went into the warm, bright kitchen. Hannah was washing the dishes. Milly put the empty plates that she was carrying on the bench beside her.

'Mum, leave those. I'll do them. You go to bed.'

'Thanks,' said Hannah and dried her hands. 'I'll say good night then.'

'Good night, Hannah,' said Michael.

'Good night.'

'I've ruined things for her this weekend,' said Milly when Hannah had gone. 'I've ruined things for everybody.'

'Yes,' said Michael, then grinned. 'But what else could you do? Besides *you* haven't ruined the weekend. The person who stole the painting did that.'

Milly looked carefully at him.

He put his hands in the air. 'It wasn't me. I didn't take it. I promise.'

Milly half-smiled and reached for a cup. 'Do you want a hot chocolate?'

'Okay.' He sat down at the table.

'So who do you think took it?' asked Milly.

'Oh,' said Michael. 'Well, of course, I don't want it to be any of the actors.'

Milly went to the refrigerator to get some milk. She poured it into a pan and put it on the stove. 'Yes, but…Well, the big question is, *Who knew the value of the painting?* Remember Polly was talking about that aunt of hers who has a second-hand shop? Polly tried to tell me the painting wasn't valuable. But maybe she knew it *was*. And she wasn't with everyone else today. Perhaps she wrapped the painting very well and hid it somewhere outside.'

Michael smiled at her. 'Maybe. But anyone could know about Isadore Richmond. I don't think I'd recognise one of his paintings, but I have heard his name before.'

Milly poured warm milk over the chocolate in the cups.

'Susan's an art teacher,' said Michael.

'Is she?' Milly took the cups to the table and sat down.

'Yes, I heard her talking to Damian about it. And Brett has an import-export business. Maybe he imports paintings. Who knows?'

'I don't even know the name of the short man with the fat fingers,' said Milly.

Michael laughed at her description. 'That's Charles.'

Milly smiled. 'We're all in this strange old house together but we really don't know much about each other, do we?'

'No,' Michael smiled back.

Milly finished her drink and said, 'I'd better go to bed.'

She opened her eyes. She could see nothing in the dark bedroom. But Hannah was still asleep in the other bed. She could hear her breathing.

Milly sat up. She was hungry. That was the trouble with serving food to everybody else. You never ate enough yourself. She stood up and felt her way to the door. She went out quietly and felt her way along the corridor towards the kitchen.

Suddenly a light cut through the dark. A second later it was gone.

Someone else was awake. Someone with a torch.

Milly stood still and listened. Her heart was beating fast. Then she laughed silently at herself. It was probably one of the actors who had been to the bathroom. Or perhaps someone else was hungry. Probably Caroline. She always seemed to be hungry.

Milly continued towards the kitchen. Then there was a noise and she stopped again. She took a second or two to recognise the sound, and then she smiled. She was right. Someone was hungry – someone had opened the refrigerator.

Milly walked to the end of the corridor. The kitchen door was half-shut. She pushed it open. For a moment, like a camera taking a photograph, Milly saw something. The refrigerator door was open towards her and hid the body of the person behind it. But, below the door in the light from the refrigerator, she saw a pair of black shoes. Then the door was quickly shut and everything was dark again.

Milly didn't move. She listened. Who was in the kitchen? And where were they now?

Suddenly the bright light of a torch shone into her eyes then came quickly towards her. She put a hand up in front of her eyes and kicked hard. Her foot hit something and she heard a cry of pain. Then a hand grabbed her neck and she was pushed up against the kitchen bench.

'Get out of the way,' a man's voice whispered angrily. His breath was hot on her face. 'Why couldn't you keep your mouth shut?'

She pushed him off her and he seemed to fall backwards. She heard a chair fall over and the torch went flying through the air, hit the table and landed on the floor. Everything went black again.

Milly ran to turn on the kitchen light. She felt along the wall in the dark. Suddenly her fingers touched another hand.

'Agh!' she screamed, and pulled her hand away. There were two of them!

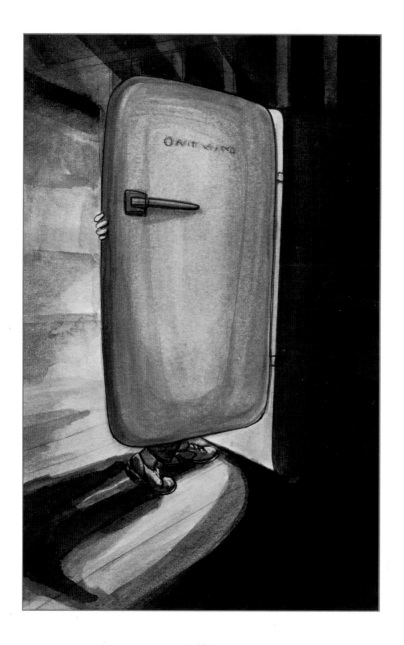

'Milly?' said Michael's voice next to her. And the kitchen light came on.

At the same moment the man behind her pushed his way out of the door. Michael and Milly both fell against the wall.

'Hey!' said Michael and ran into the dark corridor after him.

Milly slowly sank to the floor. She was shaking.

A few minutes later Michael returned. 'Are you okay?' he said and helped Milly onto a chair.

'Who was it?' she asked.

'I don't know. I couldn't see very well but I followed him into the hall. Then he completely disappeared. I turned on the lights but I couldn't find him anywhere.' Michael picked up the chair that had fallen over and then noticed something under the table. 'Hey, what's this?' he said and got down on his hands and knees to reach for it. 'Is this yours?' He held something up to show her. It was a mobile phone.

'No,' she said. 'You don't think…?'

'Maybe he dropped it.' Michael got up and pulled the chair over to sit next to Milly. He opened the phone. 'It's turned on,' he said, 'but it's set to Silent.'

Milly was still shaking but she slowly took the phone out of his hands.

She pushed a button and found the list of names and numbers stored in the phone. She began to read the list but stopped at the third name.

'Adrian B.,' she whispered. She looked at Michael. 'Adrian Bennett?'

'There's only one way to find out.'

With a shaking hand she pushed the call button and put the phone to her ear. It rang five times before Adrian's sleepy voice answered.

'Clive? What are you…? Ugh, it's half past four in the morning! What –?'

But Milly didn't wait to hear any more. She pushed the button to end the call. 'It's Clive's phone.'

'Clive?! But how –?'

'He must still be here.'

'Clive?! Don't be ridiculous,' cried Penny. 'Clive wouldn't hurt a fly.'

When Hannah had got up at six o'clock and heard about the attack on Milly she immediately sent Michael to wake the Halfords. She had woken Adrian and Susan herself and they had woken Penny. Now they had all come together in the dining room.

'So you're saying that he never left the house?' asked Adrian.

'Oh, this is crazy,' said Penny. She marched backwards and forwards across the end of the room. 'We all saw him leave.'

'But *did* we?' asked Milly quietly.

'What do you mean?' demanded Penny.

'Well, I heard a car engine start –'

'And *I* saw the car go up the hill through that window there,' interrupted Penny.

'Yes,' continued Milly. 'So did Ed, as a matter of fact – from the cottage.'

Penny interrupted again. 'And that friend of his saw Clive drive through Hill End.'

'He saw the car,' corrected Michael.

'What?'

'We all heard or saw the car,' said Milly quietly, 'but did anyone actually see Clive in it?'

Everyone looked at Penny.

'Well, no,' she said. 'I didn't actually see his face but…Oh, this is ridiculous!'

Milly said, 'Michael and I have been thinking.'

'Oh, really?' said Penny nastily.

'Did you come here with Clive on Friday?' Milly asked her.

Penny stood still and looked at her. 'Well...no. Of course, I was *going* to. Then he had a problem at work – he's an architect and the people he's working for are being very difficult – and he thought he might be late. So I came down with Brett and Anne.'

'So no one came with Clive?' asked Milly.

'No.'

'But maybe someone *was* with him,' said Milly. 'And that was the person who everyone saw drive the car away, and Clive never left the house at all.'

Penny stared at her. 'So you think Clive said to himself, "I might see a valuable painting this weekend. I think I'll hide someone in my car and then I can steal it!" That's ridiculous. I mean he's never even seen this house –'

She suddenly stopped and looked at Adrian.

'Yes, he has,' said Ed quietly.

Adrian ran a hand through his hair. 'A month ago,' he said. 'I was coming to see the house, to find out whether it would be all right for the party. But then I was ill and Clive offered to come here instead.'

'He told me he was an architect,' added Ed, 'and that he liked old houses. I went back to the cottage and left him here to have a good look around. Do you think he would recognise an Isadore Richmond painting?'

'It's possible,' said Adrian. 'Yes, it's possible.'

At the end of the room Penny sank suddenly into the nearest chair.

'Oh, Clive!' said Susan. 'What have you done?' She looked out the window. 'And where are you?'

When the other guests heard about Clive they all began looking for him. Penny thought that if he was found before the police arrived, he could explain and give back the painting and everything would be all right. They searched the house from top to bottom but there was no sign of him.

They were just putting on coats and hats and gloves to begin a search outside when the police called to say the road had opened again and they would be there soon. Ed received the call on the telephone in the hall and told the others.

'Where are the caves?' asked Adrian.

'Oh, no one can get in there,' said Ed. 'The way into the caves was closed years ago. You won't find him there.'

'We'll check anyway,' said Adrian.

So Ed and Lizzie took the guests outside to show them the way. Milly watched them go.

Then Caroline, Rod and Polly appeared, also in hats and coats.

'Well, darling,' said Caroline to Milly, 'since your little mystery has ended *ours*, we're going for a walk.' And, followed by Rod and Polly, she swept out of the front door.

Milly smiled and started back towards the kitchen. When she passed the library she saw Michael in there and stopped.

He put down his book and grinned at her. 'Have they found him yet?'

'No. Adrian thinks he may be hiding in the caves.'

Michael looked at her carefully. 'But you don't?'

'Well, I've been thinking.'

Michael laughed. 'Yes?'

'When he grabbed me in the kitchen he said, "Why couldn't you keep your mouth shut?" So he must know that *I* found out about the painting. He must be able to hear us. I think he's hiding somewhere quite close.'

Michael looked interested.

'You followed him into the hall,' said Milly, 'and then you said he disappeared, didn't you?'

'Yes. He couldn't go out through the front door. It was locked. I checked it. And I didn't hear him run upstairs. And I checked both the dining room and the sitting room and there was no one there.'

Milly walked back to the hall and Michael followed her.

The front door opened and Ed and Lizzie came in with two policemen. They took them into the sitting room.

Milly looked around the hall then walked into the dining room and back out again. She was looking carefully at the rooms.

'Clive is an architect,' she said. 'Do you think he could see something that we can't?'

She looked at the wood panelling of the wall beneath the staircase. Most houses had a cupboard under the stairs. And these stairs were so large. There must be lots of room under them. But there was no cupboard door.

'He's in there!' she said. She began to run her hands over the wall and push parts of the panelling. 'There must be a door here somewhere!'

'A door?' said Michael behind her. 'Be careful, Milly. If there is some kind of door there, he could rush out at you.' He called to the police, 'Could you come here, please?'

Suddenly a piece of panelling moved under Milly's hands and a door in the wall opened.

One of the policemen moved forward, slowly opened the door with his foot and shone his torch into the dark corridor beyond.

'Hello, sir,' he said.

And there was Clive. He was sitting on the floor next to the painting, his head in his hands. He slowly turned his face towards the open door. His eyes met Milly's.

'Got me,' he said.

The policemen dragged him out and one of them brought out the painting.

Ed went to look at the hidden door. 'I didn't even know that corridor was there,' he said.

'What's it for?' asked Milly.

Clive half-smiled at her. 'The staff,' he said. 'Didn't you think it was a long way from the kitchen to the dining room?'

'Yes,' said Milly. 'You mean the staff used to come through there?'

Clive nodded. 'That way the guests wouldn't see them.' He stared hard at her. 'They wouldn't get in anybody's way.'

'But there's no door into the kitchen,' said Lizzie.

'It's behind the refrigerator,' said Clive and gave a short laugh. 'The newest part of the kitchen.'

'So you've been hiding in there since Friday night?' asked Milly.

'Well, that wasn't the *plan*,' said Clive nastily. 'But yes. I had to take the painting the first night before Susan or someone else recognised it. I was going to be out of here before anyone woke on Saturday morning. But then the road was closed and the plan went wrong.'

The front door opened and Adrian, Susan and the other guests came into the hall.

Clive looked at the floor. The policeman beside him still held the painting.

Penny came forward. 'Clive? Why?'

Clive smiled to try to cover the look of shame on his face. 'Business is bad, Pen. I've been losing money for months and months. I was going to lose the whole business. I couldn't lose the business that my father started, could I? I needed some money quickly...When I saw the painting, I couldn't believe it. It was just hanging there. It was covered in dust. I talked a bit to Ed. I knew no one would miss it. I wouldn't even have to break in. It was going to be easy...'

'Who drove your car away?' asked Adrian.

'Toby.'

'Your brother?' said Susan, surprised.

'Yes.' Clive turned to one of the policemen. 'But I won't say that again at the police station.' He turned back to the others. 'I was going to take the painting and let myself out of the house after you had all gone to bed on Friday night and walk about a quarter of a mile up the road. Toby was going to come back and pick me up. But then the road was closed,' he said bitterly. 'I called him in the middle of the night and told him to pick me up last night but the road was closed again.' He looked back at the hidden corridor. 'It was freezing in there.'

'Come on, sir,' said one of the policemen.

The other one gave the painting to Ed. 'We'll have to send someone down to get photographs of this.' He smiled. 'So don't sell it yet.'

The policemen led Clive outside and Penny and the others followed.

Milly went to the door. Caroline, Rod and Polly were watching from a distance, then they came over and they all went inside.

Hannah was there. 'Are you all right?' she asked Milly.

'They found him!' said Caroline.

'Milly did,' said Michael. 'In there,' and he pointed at the hidden corridor.

'Aren't you clever, darling?' said Caroline. 'But we're never doing another murder weekend with you around. *Your* mystery was far too interesting!'

Everyone laughed.

'That's right,' said Michael. 'We can't beat the mystery of *Murder in the Moonlight*.'

And everyone turned to look at the painting Ed was holding.

Lizzie put a hand on Milly's arm and quietly said, 'Thank you, dear.'

'You're welcome.'

'Well, I think it's time for us to leave,' said Caroline.

And the actors began to go.

'Wait a minute,' said Milly. 'Who did kill Polly – I mean, Miss O'Halloran?'

'Don't you know?' asked Caroline. 'She doesn't know,' she said to the other actors.

Michael grinned. 'All the clues were there.'

'You're not very good at this, are you?' said Caroline.

Milly laughed. 'Just tell me.'

'Maybe I will,' said Caroline and went and put her arm around Hannah and began to lead her toward the kitchen, 'if Hannah here will make us a little bit of lunch before we go…'

Activities

Chapter 1

Before you read

A. *Look at the picture on page 8 and circle the correct answers.*
1. Why is the woman lying on the bed?
   a. Because she has been murdered.   b. Because she is asleep.
   c. Because she is tired.
2. What is this picture an advertisement for?
   a. grand beds   b. the police   c. a murder weekend

B. *Find these words in your dictionary. Use them in the sentences.*

   charming   serve   velvet   panelling

1. The old church had wood _PANELLING_ on the walls.
2. Bella thought that Cinderella was a _CHARMING_ story.
3. At the party tonight, I'm going to _SERVE_ food to the
   guests.
4. John gave Jess a red _VELVET_ box. Inside the box was a ring.

C. *Listen to Track 3 on CD1 and answer these questions.*
1. Where was Milly going?
   a. to Caves Hotel   b. to Caves House
2. Why was she going there?
   a. to play a game   b. to help her mother
3. What did Milly's mother do?
   a. She was a caterer.   b. She was a murderer.

After you read

COMPREHENSION

A. *Circle the correct answers.*
1. Where did Milly and her mother stop to buy petrol?
   a. Farnley   b. Romney   c. Wakefield
2. What did Milly buy in the café?
   a. two hot coffees   b. two hot chocolates   c. two chocolate bars
3. Which birthday was Adrian Bennett celebrating?
   a. his 30th   b. his 40th   c. his 50th
4. How many actors did Hannah have to feed for the weekend?
   a. six   b. ten   c. sixteen

B. Circle T for true or F for false for these sentences.
1. The weekend was really important for Milly's mother. (T)/ F
2. Hill End was a big town. T /(F)
3. The road going down to Caves House was steep and
   narrow. (T)/ F
4. The kitchen at Caves House was new. T /(F)

C. Complete these sentences.
1. The house was like something from a children's _____.
2. Milly thought that Ed Halford and his wife were both in their
   _____.
3. In the hall, the walls were covered with wood _____.
4. The carpet was faded and _____.

D. Write short answers to these questions.
1. What was the name of Ed Halford's wife?
   _____
2. Milly thought Ed's skin looked odd. What colour was it?
   _____
3. How many beds were in each of the downstairs bedrooms?
   _____
4. When were the Halfords coming back to welcome the guests?
   _____

LANGUAGE ACTIVITIES
A. Match the words that go together in Chapter 1.
1. petrol   a. room
2. murder   b. station
3. dining   c. cottage
4. caretaker's   d. weekend

B. Use these letters to write nouns from Chapter 1. ~~LTGHING~~ LIGHTN
1. rina: r A I N   3. linngight: l ~~IGHTH~~ LIGHTN
2. srmto: s T O R M   4. tnderhu: t H U N D E R

WHAT DO YOU THINK?
Do you think this murder weekend will go according to plan?
Why or why not?
   N O, I THINK THAt WILL GOING TO BE
A TROU BLE .

Chapters 2 and 3

Before you read

A. Look at the picture on page 15 and circle the correct answers.
1. What room are all these people in?
   a. the dining room   b. the library   c.)the kitchen
2. Milly is standing at the table. What is she holding?
   a. a pot   (b.) a knife   c. an apple

B. Find these words in your dictionary. Use them in the sentences.

   silently   pretend   wrapped   dramatic
1. Olivia __WRAPPED__ Jill's birthday present in pretty paper.
2. The students walked __SILENTLY__ into the classroom.
3. There was a __DRAMATIC__ silence. Then Henry said, 'I did it!'
4. Those two boys like to __PRETEND__ they are monsters.

C. Listen to Track 4 on CD1 and answer these questions.
1. What did Hannah call 'horrible' because it wasn't working well?
   a. the stove   b. the refrigerator
2. How was Hannah feeling?
   a. happy and calm   b. nervous and angry
3. Whose voice did Milly hear coming from the corridor?
   a. Lizzie's   b. Ed's

After you read

COMPREHENSION
A. Circle the correct answers.
1. Which actor wore a blood-red scarf?
   a.) Caroline   b.) Andy   c. Polly
2. Who juggled the apples?
   a. Andy   b. Bernie   c.) Michael
3. Why was the road closed?
   a.) Because there was ice on it.   b. Because it was too steep.
   c. Because it was too narrow.
4. What was missing from the dining room at breakfast time?
   a. a tablecloth   b.) a painting   c. a curtain

B. Circle T for true or F for false for these sentences.
1. Hannah set the table.   T /**F**
2. Adrian's wife Susan had blonde hair.   **T** / F
3. The actors ate breakfast in the kitchen.   T /**F**
4. Polly played the detective.   T /**F**

C. Complete these sentences.
1. Caroline pretended to be Lady ___Bird___.
2. On the last few steps of the staircase lay the body of
   ___Brook___.
3. Milly helped Lizzie to make the ___beds___.
4. With the road closed, no one was allowed in or ___out___.

D. Write short answers to these questions.
1. Which guest had to leave at ten o'clock at night?

   _____

2. What song did everyone sing?

   _____

3. At breakfast, who asked Milly to thank her mother for the
   wonderful meal the night before?

   _____

4. What did the detective say they had to search the house for?

   _____

LANGUAGE ACTIVITIES
A. Match each word with its opposite from Chapters 2 and 3.
1. horrible   a. ancient
2. modern   b. tall
3. short   c. thin
4. fat   d. wonderful

B. Write the missing vowels to make nouns from Chapters 2 and 3.
1. sc A rf   3. pyj A m A s
2. c _ _ t   4. dr E ss

WHAT DO YOU THINK?
Why do you think someone would take the painting from the
dining room?

_____

Chapters 4 and 5

Before you read

A. Look at the picture on page 34 and circle the correct answers.

1. Where is Milly?
   a. outside, on a stone bridge   b. inside the caretaker's cottage
   c. outside, on a wooden bridge
2. What kind of day is it?
   a. hot   b. rainy   c. cold

B. Find these words in your dictionary. Use them in the sentences.

   local   second-hand   moonlight   broke in

1. I bought this old armchair from a _SECOND-HAND_ shop for €50.
2. It was a lovely night for a walk in the _MOONLIGHT_
3. The robbers _BROKE IN_ through the bathroom window
   and stole all our cash.
4. There are some great restaurants in the _LOCAL_ area.

C. Listen to Track 5 on CD1 and answer these questions.

1. Why did Ed and Lizzie live in the caretaker's cottage?
   a. Because they were caretakers.
   b. Because they only needed a small place.
2. Where did Ed's mother take him to live when he was very young?
   a. Farnley   b. Australia
3. When did Ed come back to Caves House?
   a. about twenty-five years ago   b. about thirty-five years ago

After you read

COMPREHENSION

A. Circle the correct answers.

1. Whose aunt had a second-hand shop?
   a. Milly's   b. Polly's   c. Caroline's
2. Why did Milly keep thinking about the stolen painting?
   a. Because she liked the painting.
   b. Because she took the painting.
   c. Because she painted the painting.
3. Where did Milly find information about Isadore Richmond?
   a. in an old book   b. in an email   c. in an old newspaper
4. When did Hannah have to serve afternoon tea?
   a. at three o'clock   b. at four o'clock   c. at five o'clock

B. Circle T for true or F for false for these sentences.
1. Hannah told Milly not to talk to the guests about
   the painting.   T / F
2. Ed had always known who'd painted the missing painting. T / F
3. The painting could have been worth a lot of money.   T / F
4. Lizzie wanted to ruin Mr Bennett's birthday party.   T / F

C. Complete these sentences.
1. Ed's father had made a complete list of everything in the
   Green Book Oln
2. Ed had an old book with a green cloth _____.
3. Susan brought the camera to Milly and showed her a
   PRoTuo .
4. The police couldn't come until the road was _CLOSE_ .

D. Write short answers to these questions.
1. Who wasn't well – in fact, was very ill?

   _____

2. What was the name of the missing painting?

   _____

3. In whose room did Milly find a blue case big enough for the
   painting?

   _____

4. Who had locked the doors of Caves House after dinner the night
   before?

   _____

LANGUAGE ACTIVITIES
A. Write the correct prepositions in the spaces.
   onto   on   around   along
1. Rod put on his detective's hat and walked _ALoNb_ the
   room.
2. Hannah sank _oNto_ her bed.
3. Milly walked quickly _ALoVN_ the road.
4. Milly knocked _oN_ the cottage door.

B. Write the missing vowels to make verbs from Chapters 4 and 5.
1. _i nv E st _i g L t i_   3. s _E_ rch
2. ch _i_ ck   4. l _o_ k

WHAT DO YOU THINK?
Do you think that Ed should have called the police? Why or why not?

_____

Chapter 6

Before you read

A. Look at the picture on page 49 and circle the correct answers.
1. When is this?
    a. in the middle of the day   b. in the middle of the night
    c. in the afternoon
2. Why can't we see who is looking into the refrigerator?
    a. Because the person is behind the refrigerator door.
    b. Because there is no light.   c. Because the light is too bright.

B. Find these words in your dictionary. Use them in the sentences.

   torch   probably   shaking   architect

1. Paul will _____ win this race. He's the fastest runner.
2. Mal's hands were _____ when he met Queen Elizabeth.
3. Liz talked to her _____ about her ideas for the new house.
4. I turned on my _____ so that I could see where to go.

C. Listen to Track 6 on CD1 and answer these questions.
1. Where did Michael catch up with Milly?
    a. in the dining room   b. in the corridor
2. What was Hannah doing in the kitchen?
    a. washing the dishes   b. eating her dinner
3. Who did Michael think had ruined the weekend?
    a. Milly   b. the person who stole the painting

After you read

COMPREHENSION
A. Circle the correct answers.
1. When she made hot chocolates, where did Milly get the milk from?
    a. the cupboard   b. the table   c. the refrigerator
2. What subject did Susan teach?
    a. art   b. English   c. history
3. What was the name of the short man with the fat fingers?
    a. Damian   b. Brett   c. Charles
4. Why did Milly get out of bed in the middle of the night?
    a. Because she'd heard a noise.   b. Because she was hungry.
    c. Because she was cold.

B. Circle T for true or F for false for these sentences.
1. Clive dropped his mobile phone in the kitchen.   T / F
2. Milly rang Adrian with Clive's phone.   T / F
3. Clive left in his car on Friday night.   T / F
4. Clive had been to Caves House before.   T / F

C. Complete these sentences.
1. Clive's phone was turned on but it was set to _____.
2. It was possible Clive would recognise an Isadore Richmond
_____.
3. Michael had followed Clive into the hall, then Clive had
_____.
4. Michael hadn't heard Clive run _____.

D. Write short answers to these questions.
1. What did Clive do for a living?
_____
2. Who called to say the road was open again and they would be there soon?
_____
3. Who used the hidden corridor in the past?
_____
4. Who was Toby?
_____

LANGUAGE ACTIVITIES
A. Write the correct prepositions in the spaces.
    under   in   towards   over
1. Milly poured warm milk _____ the chocolate in the cups.
2. Milly continued _____ the kitchen.
3. Michael noticed something _____ the table.
4. Michael put his hands _____ the air.

B. Write the missing vowels to make nouns from Chapter 6.
1. c _ rr _ d _ r   3. b _ thr _ _ m
2. k _ tch _ n   4. h _ ll

WHAT DO YOU THINK?
Do you think Milly was a good detective? Why or why not?
_____

Glossary

adj. adjective; *adv.* adverb; *n.* noun; *v.* verb

accuse /əˈkjuːz/ *v.* to say that someone has done
  something wrong
actor /ˈæktə/ *n.* a person who acts in plays or films
actually /ˈæktʃuəli/ *adv.* really
architect /ˈɑːkɪˌtekt/ *n.* a person whose job is to design buildings
art /ɑːt/ *n.* beautiful things that people make, such as paintings
  and drawings
artist /ˈɑːtɪst/ *n.* a person who does paintings or drawings or
  makes other pieces of art
believe /bɪˈliːv/ *v.* to feel sure that something is true
bench /bentʃ/ *n.* a long table for people to do work on
bin /bɪn/ *n.* a container to put things in, usually rubbish
blood /blʌd/ *n.* the red liquid that flows inside your body
break in /breɪk ɪn/ *v.* to illegally enter a building or house
breathe /briːð/ *v.* to take air into your body through your nose or
  mouth; to speak in a quiet, dramatic way
caretaker /ˈkeəˌteɪkə/ *n.* a person whose job is to live in or near a
  building and look after it
carrot /ˈkærət/ *n.* a long, hard, orange vegetable
caterer /ˈkeɪtərə/ *n.* a person whose job is to provide food for
  large groups of people, for example at parties
catering /ˈkeɪtərɪŋ/ *n.* the job of providing food for large groups
  of people
cave /keɪv/ *n.* a large hole in the side of a mountain or under
  the ground
charming /ˈtʃɑːmɪŋ/ *adj.* behaving in a way that makes people
  like you
cheeky /ˈtʃiːki/ *adj.* behaving or speaking in a way that does not
  show respect for someone, especially for an older person
clue /kluː/ *n.* something that helps you find the answer to a
  problem or puzzle

corridor /'kɒrɪˌdɔː/ *n.* a long narrow room that leads to other rooms

cottage /'kɒtɪdʒ/ *n.* a little house

counter /'kaʊntə/ *n.* the table that the shopkeeper stands behind in a shop

cover /'kʌvə/ *v.* to be over something else; to hide something *n.* something that goes outside or over something else

craggy /'krægi/ *adj.* with lots of sharp points and edges

curtains /'kɜːtnz/ *n.* large pieces of cloth that cover a window

darling /'dɑːlɪŋ/ *n.* a word you call someone who you love or like a lot

death /deθ/ *n.* the end of life

demand /dɪ'mɑːnd/ *v.* to ask a question in a forceful way

details /'diːteɪlz/ *n.* pieces of information about something

discover /dɪ'skʌvə/ *v.* to find for the first time

dramatic /drə'mætɪk/ *adj.* exciting and unusual

dramatically /drə'mætɪkli/ *adv.* in a way that is exciting and unusual so as to impress people

dust /dʌst/ *n.* very small pieces of dirt that fall onto the flat surfaces in a room over time if it is not cleaned very often

faded /feɪdɪd/ *adj.* having lost colour or brightness over a length of time

feather /'feðə/ *n.* one of the long coloured things that cover a bird's body

fireplace /'faɪəˌpleɪs/ *n.* the place in a room where you can have a fire to make the room warm

freezing /'friːzɪŋ/ *adj.* very cold

ghost /ɡəʊst/ *n.* the spirit or form of a dead person that someone thinks they can see

glare /ɡleə/ *v.* to look at someone or something in an angry way

gloves /ɡlʌvz/ *n.* cloth covers for the hands to keep them warm

grab /ɡræb/ *v.* to take hold of something quickly with your hand

grand /ɡrænd/ *adj.* looking big and important

grin /grɪn/ *n.* a smile

    v. to have a big smile on your face, usually with your teeth showing

gunshot /ˈɡʌnˌʃɒt/ *n.* the loud noise that a gun makes

hall /hɔːl/ *n.* a long room in a building that has doors to a number of other rooms

import-export /ˈɪmpɔːt ˈekspɔːt/ *adj.* buying things from or selling things to people in other countries

interrupt /ˌɪntəˈrʌpt/ *v.* to say or do something that stops what someone else is saying or doing

investigate /ɪnˈvestɪˌɡeɪt/ *v.* to try and find out the facts about something

juggle /ˈdʒʌɡl/ *v.* to throw a number of things up in the air at the same time and catch them over and over again

jut /dʒʌt/ *v.* to point out further than other parts of a thing

lightning /ˈlaɪtnɪŋ/ *n.* bright light that appears in the sky during a storm

local /ˈləʊkl/ *adj.* from the nearby area

moonlight /ˈmuːnˌlaɪt/ *n.* light coming from the moon at night

murder /ˈmɜːdə/ *n.* the crime of killing someone

    v. to kill someone not by accident

nasty /ˈnɑːsti/ *adj.* very unpleasant

necklace /ˈnekləs/ *n.* a pretty thing made from metal, jewels or beads that you wear around your neck

odd /ɒd/ *adj.* strange, unusual

painting /ˈpeɪntɪŋ/ *n.* a picture that someone has made using a brush and paint

panelling /ˈpænlɪŋ/ *n.* flat pieces of wood that together make up the wall of a room

pretend /prɪˈtend/ *v.* to try to make someone believe that you are doing something when you are not really doing it

probably /ˈprɒbəbli/ *adv.* We use *probably* to say that we think something is likely to be true.

pyjamas /pəˈdʒɑːməz/ *n.* loose trousers and a loose jacket that you wear in bed

refrigerator /rɪ'frɪdʒəˌreɪtə/ *n.* a machine like a box that uses electricity to keep food and drink cold

ridiculous /rɪ'dɪkjʊləs/ *adj.* very foolish or silly

rubbish /'rʌbɪʃ/ *n.* things you do not want and throw away

ruin /'ruːɪn/ *v.* to spoil or badly damage something

scraps /skræps/ *n.* pieces of food that are not used when cooking and so are thrown away

script /skrɪpt/ *n.* a book or collection of pages containing the words an actor should say

second-hand /'sekənd hænd/ *adj.* already owned by someone else, not new

serve /sɜːv/ *v.* to bring food or drink for people

shake /ʃeɪk/ *v.* to move quickly up and down or from side to side, perhaps because you are cold or afraid

sheet /ʃiːt/ *n.* a large square piece of thin cloth that you sleep on or cover yourself with in bed; a piece of paper

silence /'saɪləns/ *n.* no noise; a time when everything is quiet

silent /'saɪlənt/ *adj.* not speaking or making noise

silently /'saɪləntli/ *adv.* without speaking or making noise

solve /sɒlv/ *v.* to find the answer

staff /stɑːf/ *n.* the people who work in a place

staircase /'steəˌkeɪs/ *n.* a set of steps in a building going up and down between floors

steep /stiːp/ *adj.* going upwards or downwards at a high angle, not flat

stove /stəʊv/ *n.* something that you can cook or heat food on

swept /swept/ past tense of **sweep** *v.* to walk in a quick and forceful way

tablecloth /'teɪblˌklɒθ/ *n.* a large kind of sheet that you put over a table

thunder /'θʌndə/ *n.* the loud noise that you hear after a flash of lightning, especially during a storm

torch /tɔːtʃ/ *n.* a small electric light that you can hold in your hand to see in the dark

turban /'tɜːbən/ *n.* a kind of hat made of cloth that goes around and around a person's head

valuable /'væljʊbl/ *adj.* worth a lot of money

velvet /'velvɪt/ *n.* a kind of soft material

whisper /'wɪspə/ *v.* to speak in a very soft voice, using only your breath

wine /waɪn/ *n.* a red or white alcoholic drink made from grapes

worn /wɔːn/ *adj.* looking damaged after being used a lot for a long time

worry /'wʌri/ *v.* to be unhappy because you think something bad will happen

wrap /ræp/ *v.* to put cloth or paper closely around something, to cover it

Murder Weekned
Activities: Answer Key

Chapter 1
Before you read

A. 1. a, 2. c   B. 1. panelling,
2. charming, 3. serve, 4. velvet
C. 1. b, 2. b, 3. a

After you read
Comprehension

A. 1. c, 2. b, 3. b, 4. a   B. 1. T, 2. F, 3. T,
4. F   C. 1. book, 2. sixties, 3. panelling,
4. worn   D. 1. Lizzie, 2. grey, 3. two,
4. at six thirty

Language activities

A. 1. b, 2. d, 3. a, 4. c   B. 1. rain,
2. storm, 3. lightning, 4. thunder

What do you think?
Students' own answers

Chapters 2 and 3
Before you read

A. 1. c, 2. b   B. 1. wrapped, 2. silently,
3. dramatic, 4. pretend   C. 1. a, 2. b,
3. b

After you read
Comprehension

A. 1. a, 2. c, 3. a, 4. b   B. 1. F, 2. T, 3. T,
4. F   C. 1. Dunsany, 2. Miss O'Halloran,
3. beds, 4. out   D. 1. Clive, 2. *Happy
Birthday*, 3. Adrian, 4. the knife

Language activities

A. 1. d, 2. a, 3. b, 4. c   B. 1. scarf,
2. coat, 3. pyjamas, 4. dress

What do you think?
Students' own answers

Chapters 4 and 5
Before you read

A. 1. a, 2. c   B. 1. second-hand,
2. moonlight, 3. broke in, 4. local
C. 1. b, 2. b, 3. a

After you read
Comprehension

A. 1. b, 2. a, 3. c, 4. b   B. 1. T, 2. F, 3. T,
4. F   C. 1. house, 2. cover,
3. photograph, 4. open   D. 1. Ed,
2. Murder in the Moonlight, 3. Penny
Harrington's, 4. Adrian

Language activities

A. 1. around, 2. onto, 3. along, 4. on
B. 1. investigate, 2. check, 3. search,
4. look

What do you think?
Students' own answers

Chapter 6
Before you read

A. 1. b, 2. a   B. 1. probably, 2. shaking,
3. architect, 4. torch   C. 1. b, 2. a, 3. b

After you read
Comprehension

A. 1. c, 2. a, 3. c, 4. b   B. 1. T, 2. T, 3. F,
4. T   C. 1. Silent, 2. painting,
3. disappeared, 4. upstairs   D. 1. He was
an architect. 2. the police, 3. the staff,
4. Clive's brother

Language activities

A. 1. over, 2. towards, 3. under, 4. in
B. 1. corridor, 2. kitchen, 3. bathroom,
4. hall

What do you think?
Students' own answers